101 Things To Do With A Cake Mix

101 Things To Do With A Cake Mix

BY
STEPHANIE ASHCRAFT

Gibbs Smith, Publisher
Salt Lake City

First Edition
08 07 06 05 04   20 19 18 17 16 15 14 13

Text © 2002 by Stephanie Ashcraft

Published by
Gibbs Smith, Publisher
P.O. Box 667
Layton, Utah 84041

Orders: (1-800) 748-5439
www.gibbs-smith.com

Edited by Suzanne Gibbs Taylor
Designed and produced by Kurt Wahlner
Printed and bound in Korea

Library of Congress Cataloging-in-Publication Data

Ashcraft, Stephanie.
101 things to do with a cake mix/Stephanie Ashcraft. — 1st ed.
          p. cm.
ISBN 1-58685-217-5
I. Cake. I. Title: One hundred and one things to do with a cake mix.
II. Title
TX 771 .A82 2002
641.8'653—dc21

                    2002005353

DEDICATION

Dedicated to my mother, Shirley Dircks, who taught me that anything could be made with a cake mix. Her excitement for life and enduring love for everyone are wonderful examples for me.

To my husband, Ivan, for all of his support and encouragement.

CONTENTS

Helpful Hints 9

Brownies and Bars

Cookies

Fruity Cakes

Fancy Cakes

Bundt Cakes

Muffins and Breads

Children's Delights

HELPFUL HINTS

 Always beat cake batter with an electric mixer for at least 2 minutes.

Always grease and flour the cake pan, or spray it with oil—even when the recipe doesn't call for it.

Bake cakes on the middle oven rack, never on the top or bottom racks.

For chewier cookies and bars, take them out of the oven just as they begin to look golden and let them cool on or in the pan.

For recipes using gelatin, make sure the gelatin is completely dissolved in hot water before adding any cold water.

When using fresh fruit, dip it in pineapple, orange, or lemon juice so it won't change color.

To see if a cake is done, insert a toothpick into the center—if it comes out clean, it's done. If the cake springs back when touched, that also means it's done.

The first time you try a recipe, check the cake five minutes before its minimum cooking time ends—each oven heats differently.

For best results, use glass or stoneware baking dishes.

BROWNIES
AND BARS

WHITE-CHOCOLATE FUDGE BARS

1 **chocolate fudge cake mix**
2 **eggs**
1/3 **cup oil**
$^3/_4$ cup **white chocolate chips**

Preheat oven to 350 degrees.

Mix together cake mix, eggs, and oil. Stir in white chocolate chips.
Mixture will be stiff. Press dough into a greased 9 x 13-inch pan.

Bake 14–16 minutes.

Serve warm or at room temperature. Can be topped with favorite frosting, if desired.

LEMON SQUARES

1	**lemon cake mix**
2	**eggs**
1/3 cup	**oil**
	powdered sugar

Preheat oven to 350 degrees.

In a bowl, mix together cake mix, eggs, and oil. Mixture will be stiff. Spread the mixture evenly into a greased 9 x 13-inch pan.

Bake 13–15 minutes until slightly golden on top.

Cool, then sprinkle powdered sugar over the squares.

PEANUT BUTTER-CHOCOLATE CHIP BARS

1 **chocolate chip** or **yellow cake mix**
2 **eggs**
$^1/_3$ cup **vegetable oil**
$^1/_2$ cup **chunky peanut butter**
1 cup **chocolate chips**

Preheat oven to 350 degrees.

Mix together cake mix, eggs, and oil. Mix in peanut butter. Stir in chocolate chips. Pat the mixture into a 9 x 13-inch pan.

Bake 14–17 minutes, or until golden brown.

Note: Using chunky peanut butter will make your friends and family think you spent all day chopping nuts.

CHEESECAKE BARS
(GRANDMA DIRCKS' SPECIALTY)

Bottom Layer:

1	**yellow cake mix**
1 stick	**margarine**, melted and cooled
1	**egg**, beaten

Top Layer:

1 pound	**powdered sugar**
2	**eggs**, beaten
8 ounces	**cream cheese**
1 teaspoon	**vanilla**

Preheat oven to 350 degrees.

Add cake mix and beaten egg to melted margarine. Spread mixture into bottom of a greased-and-floured 9 x 13-inch pan.

In a separate bowl, mix together powdered sugar, eggs, softened cream cheese, and vanilla until smooth. Spread mixture over bottom layer.

Bake 30–35 minutes.

CHOCOLATE SQUARES

1 **chocolate cake mix**
2 **eggs**
$^1/_3$ cup **oil**

Preheat oven to 350 degrees.

In a bowl, mix together cake mix, eggs, and oil. Mixture will be stiff. Spread the mixture evenly into a greased 9 x 13-inch pan.

Bake 13–16 minutes, until the brownies reach the desired consistency.

CHEWY BROWNIES

1 **chocolate cake mix**
$^1/_2$ cup **margarine**, softened
3 **eggs**
$^3/_4$ cup **semisweet chocolate chips**
$^1/_2$ cup **chopped nuts**

Preheat oven to 350 degrees.

Mix together cake mix, margarine, and eggs until the cake mix is completely absorbed. Stir in chips and nuts. Press the stiff dough evenly into a greased 9 x 13-inch pan.

Bake 26–30 minutes. When cooled, cut into squares and serve.

CHERRY CHIP SQUARES

1 **cherry chip cake mix**
2 **eggs**
$^1/_3$ cup **oil**

Preheat oven to 350 degrees.

In a bowl, mix cake mix, eggs, and oil together. Mixture will be stiff. Spread the mixture evenly into a greased 9 x 13-inch pan.

Bake at 350 degrees for 13–17 minutes, or until lightly brown on top. Serve warm or at room temperature.

CHEWY LEMON BARS

1 **lemon cake mix**
1 **egg**
$^1/_2$ cup **butter**, melted
3 $^3/_4$ cups **powdered sugar**
2 **eggs**, beaten
8 ounces **cream cheese**, softened
1 teaspoon **vanilla**

Preheat oven to 350 degrees.

Mix together cake mix, egg, and butter. Spread into a greased 9 x 13-inch pan.

In a separate bowl, mix together powdered sugar, beaten eggs, softened cream cheese, and vanilla until smooth. Spread mixture over bottom layer.

Bake 30–40 minutes, until top layer turns a light golden brown.

STRAWBERRY SQUARES

1 **strawberry cake mix**
2 **eggs**
$^1/_3$ cup **oil**
1 $^1/_2$ tablespoons **milk**
1 cup **powdered sugar**

Preheat oven to 350 degrees.

Mix together cake mix, eggs, and oil until stiff. Spread the dough evenly in a 9 x 13-inch pan.

Bake the squares 14–16 minutes.

Mix the milk and powdered sugar. Drizzle the glaze over the squares. Serve warm or at room temperature. Also tasty right out of the oven.

PEANUT BUTTER BROWNIES

Cake:

I	**yellow** or **white cake mix**
$^1/_3$ cup	**oil**
2	**eggs**
$^2/_3$ cup	**chunky peanut butter**

Glaze:

I $^1/_2$ tablespoons	**milk**
I cup	**powdered sugar**

Preheat oven to 350 degrees.

Mix together cake mix, oil, and eggs. Mixture should be stiff and all the powder should be mixed into the dough. Stir in peanut butter.

Bake 14–16 minutes, until golden brown on top.

Mix together powdered sugar and milk. Drizzle powdered-sugar glaze over top while still warm.

CHEWY CHOCOLATE CHIP BARS

  1 **yellow or white cake mix**
  2 **eggs**
$^1/_3$ cup **oil**
$^3/_4$ cup **chocolate chips**

Preheat oven to 350 degrees.

Mix together cake mix, eggs, and oil. Stir the mixture until all the powder is evenly mixed in. Stir in the chips. Spread the mixture evenly in a 9 x 13-inch pan.

Bake 14–16 minutes, or until light golden brown on top.

Serve warm or at room temperature.

GOOEY BARS

1 **yellow cake mix**
$^3/_4$ cup **nuts** (optional)
1 stick **butter** or **margarine**
1 box (1 pound) **powdered sugar**
8 ounces **cream cheese**
1 **egg**

Mix together cake mix, nuts, and butter. Press into a greased 9 x 13-inch pan.

Mix together powdered sugar, egg, and cream cheese. Blend thoroughly. Spread over bottom layer.

Bake 35–45 minutes, or until golden brown.

Cool and cut into small squares.

HEAVENLY BROWNIES

Bottom Layer:

1 **chocolate cake mix**
$^1/_2$ cup **butter**, melted
1 **egg**
$^1/_2$ cup **chopped pecans** (optional)

Top Layer:

1 box (1 pound) **powdered sugar**
8 ounces **cream cheese**
2 **eggs**

Preheat oven to 350 degrees.

Mix dry cake mix, butter, and 1 egg. Add pecans if desired. Spread into a greased 9 x 13-inch pan.

Beat powdered sugar, cream cheese, and remaining 2 eggs together; spread over bottom layer.

Bake 40–50 minutes, or until golden brown.

APPLE-CINNAMON BARS

1 **yellow cake mix**
1 stick **butter** or **margarine**, softened
$^1/_3$ cup **coconut**
4 medium **apples**
$^1/_2$ cup **sugar**
1 teaspoon **cinnamon**
1 cup **sour cream**
1 **egg**

Preheat oven to 350 degrees.

Cut butter into dry cake mix with fork or pastry blender until mixture is crumbly. Mix in coconut. Pat mixture into ungreased 9 x 13-inch pan. Pat slightly up on the edges.

Bake 10 minutes.

Peel, core, and slice apples. Arrange apple slices on warm crust. Mix sugar and cinnamon; sprinkle on top of apples.

Beat the egg with a wire whisk. Blend sour cream into the egg. Drizzle mixture over apples.

Bake 25 minutes, or until edges are lightly golden. Serve warm with a scoop of vanilla ice cream.

BUTTERSCOTCH CHIP BARS

1 **yellow cake mix**
2 **eggs**
$^1/_3$ cup **oil**
$^3/_4$ cup **butterscotch chips**

Preheat oven to 350 degrees.

Mix together cake mix, eggs, and oil. Stir in butterscotch chips until stiff. Press dough into a lightly greased 9 x 13-inch pan.

Bake 13–16 minutes.

REESE'S PIECES BARS

1 **yellow cake mix**
2 **eggs**
$^1/_3$ cup **oil**
1 $^1/_2$ cups **Reese's Pieces**

Preheat oven to 350 degrees. In a large bowl, mix together cake mix, eggs, and oil until cake mix is dissolved. Mix Reese's Pieces into dough.

Bake 13–17 minutes in a greased 9 x 13-inch pan until golden brown.

PUMPKIN PIE BARS

Bottom Layer:

I can (29 ounces)	**pumpkin**
I cup	**milk**
I cup	**sugar**
2	**eggs**
I teaspoon	**cinnamon**
$^1/_2$ teaspoon	**nutmeg**
$^1/_2$ teaspoon	**ginger**
$^1/_2$ teaspoon	**salt**

Top Layer:

I	**yellow cake mix**
$^3/_4$ cup	**walnuts**, chopped
I $^1/_2$ sticks	**butter**, melted

Preheat oven to 350 degrees.

In large bowl, mix together all ingredients for the bottom layer. Spread mixture into a glass 9 x 13-inch pan.

Pat yellow cake mix over bottom layer. Spread walnuts over dry mix. Cover dry mix with melted butter.

Bake 45–55 minutes, or until golden brown.

CREAM CHEESE BARS

Crust:

　　　　　I **yellow cake mix**
　　　　　I **egg**
　　　$^1/_3$ cup **oil**

Filling:

　　　8 ounces **cream cheese**
　　　　$^1/_3$ cup **sugar**
　　I teaspoon **lemon juice**
　　　　　I **egg**

Preheat oven to 350 degrees.

Mix together cake mix, egg, and oil until crumbly. Set aside I cup of crust mixture for topping. Pat rest of dough lightly into a greased 9 x 13-inch pan.

Bake 15 minutes.

In a separate bowl, beat together cream cheese, sugar, lemon juice, and egg until smooth. Spread evenly over baked layer. Sprinkle with reserved crust mixture.

Bake 15 minutes longer. Cool and cut into bars.

GERMAN CHOCOLATE BARS

Bottom Layer:

1 **German chocolate cake mix**
1 cup **quick oatmeal**
1 stick **butter,** softened
1 **egg**

Top Layer:

8 ounces **cream cheese**
2 **eggs**
1 package (16 ounces) **coconut-pecan frosting**

Preheat oven to 350 degrees.

With a fork, mix together cake mix, oatmeal, butter, and egg until crumbly. Set aside two cups of mixture. Press rest of dough into a greased 9 x 13-inch pan.

In a separate bowl, beat together cream cheese and eggs until smooth. Mix frosting into cream-cheese mixture. Spread over crust. Sprinkle reserved oatmeal mixture over cream-cheese layer.

Bake 40-45 minutes, or until done.

COOKIES

REESE'S COOKIES

1 **chocolate cake mix**
2 **eggs**
$^1/_3$ cup **vegetable oil**
1 bag small-size **Reese's Peanut Butter Cups**

Preheat oven to 350 degrees.

Mix together cake mix, eggs, and oil in a bowl until all the cake powder is absorbed. Place a peanut butter cup in the center of a ball of dough. Make sure the cup is completely covered with dough.

Bake cookies 8–10 minutes, or until done. Remove from pan and cool.

CHEWY LEMON COOKIES

I	**lemon cake mix**
2 cups	**whipped topping**
2	**eggs**
	powdered sugar

Mix together cake mix, whipped topping, and eggs. Refrigerate 2 hours.

Preheat oven to 350 degrees.

Lightly grease a cookie pan. Roll cookie dough into small balls, then roll balls in powdered sugar. Space balls evenly on cookie sheet.

Bake 6–8 minutes. Remove from pan and cool.

SWEET DELIGHTS

1 **cake mix**, any flavor
$^1/_4$ cup **light-brown sugar**
$^1/_3$ cup **oil**
2 **eggs**
$^3/_4$ cup **chocolate chips**

Preheat oven to 375 degrees.

Mix together cake mix, brown sugar, oil, and eggs. Stir in chocolate chips.

Drop dough balls onto greased cookie sheet. Bake 8–10 minutes, or until golden brown. Remove from pan and cool.

CHOCOLATE CHIP COOKIES

1 **yellow cake mix**
1/2 cup **butter**, softened
1 teaspoon **vanilla**
2 **eggs**
2/3 cup **chocolate chips**
1/2 cup **chopped nuts**

Preheat oven to 350 degrees.

Mix half the cake mix with butter, vanilla, and eggs until smooth. Stir in chocolate chips and nuts. Stir in the rest of the cake mix until absorbed. Use cookie scoop to drop dough onto an ungreased cookie sheet.

Bake cookies 10–12 minutes. Remove from pan and place on nonstick cooling rack to cool.

TOUCH O' HONEY

　　　1 **cake mix**, any flavor
　　　2 **eggs**
　1/3 cup **honey**
　1/3 cup **margarine**
　1/2 cup **flour**

Preheat oven to 350 degrees.

Blend half of cake mix, eggs, honey, margarine, and flour, then beat until fluffy, mixing in rest of cake mix. Roll into small balls.

Bake on ungreased cookie sheet 10–12 minutes. Remove from pan and cool.

PEANUT BUTTER-KISS COOKIES

1 **yellow cake mix**
2 **eggs**
$^1/_3$ cup **oil**
$^3/_4$ cup **peanut butter**
1 package **Hershey's Kisses**

Preheat oven to 350 degrees.

Mix together cake mix, eggs, and oil until mixture reaches brownie consistency. Mix peanut butter into the dough. Drop balls of dough onto a lightly greased pan. Place an unwrapped chocolate kiss in the center of each ball.

Bake 10 minutes, or until light golden brown. Remove from pan and cool.

EASY SNICKER DOODLES

1 **yellow cake mix**
1 teaspoon **vanilla extract**
$^1/_3$ cup **vegetable oil**
2 **eggs**
$^1/_2$ cup **sugar**
2 teaspoons **ground cinnamon**

Preheat oven to 375 degrees.

Mix sugar and cinnamon; set aside.

In a bowl mix together cake mix, vanilla, oil, and eggs until dough is formed. Shape cookie dough into 1-inch balls. Roll balls in sugar-cinnamon mixture.

Bake 8–10 minutes, or until golden brown. Remove from pan and cool.

BUTTERFINGER COOKIES

1 **yellow** or **chocolate cake mix**
2 **eggs**
¹/₃ cup **vegetable oil**
1 large **Butterfinger candy bar**

Preheat oven to 350 degrees.

Mix together cake mix, eggs, and oil until powder is completely dissolved into dough.

Chop Butterfinger into tiny pieces, then mix into dough. Drop dough in small balls onto greased cookie sheet.

Bake 10–12 minutes, or until lightly golden. Do not overbake. Remove from pan and cool.

QUICK AND EASY
PEANUT BUTTER COOKIES

I	**yellow cake mix**
2	**eggs**
$^1/_3$ cup	**oil**
$^3/_4$ cup	**crunchy peanut butter**
	sugar

Preheat oven to 350 degrees.

Mix together cake mix, eggs, and oil until powder is completely dissolved into dough. Stir in peanut butter.

Drop balls of dough into a small bowl of sugar, then place on a greased cookie sheet. Press fork horizontally and then vertically across each ball to flatten.

Bake 10–12 minutes, or until golden. Remove from pan and cool.

CHOCOLATE BUTTERSCOTCH-CHIP COOKIES

1	**chocolate cake mix**
2	**eggs**
1/3 cup	**vegetable oil**
1 cup	**butterscotch chips**

Preheat oven to 350 degrees.

Mix together cake mix, eggs, and oil in a large bowl until mix is dissolved. Mix butterscotch chips into dough. Drop balls of dough onto a greased baking sheet.

Bake 9–12 minutes, until golden brown. Remove from pan and cool.

EASY M&M COOKIES

1 **white cake mix**
2 **eggs**
1/3 cup **vegetable oil**
1 1/4 cup **plain M&Ms**

Preheat oven to 350 degrees.

Mix together cake mix, eggs, and oil in a large bowl until mix is dissolved. Mix M&Ms into dough.

Drop balls of dough onto greased baking sheet.

Bake 9–12 minutes, until golden brown. Remove from pan and cool.

CHOCO SANDWICH COOKIES

1 **chocolate cake mix**
2 cups **whipped topping**
2 **eggs**
1 can **vanilla frosting** (16 ounces)
powdered sugar

Mix together cake mix, whipped topping and eggs. Chill in refrigerator for two hours.

Preheat oven to 350 degrees.

Roll cookie dough into small balls, and then roll balls in powdered sugar. Space dough balls evenly on a lightly greased cookie sheet.

Bake 7–10 minutes. Cool. Spread vanilla frosting between two cookies and serve.

FRUITY
CAKES

CHERRY PIE-FILLING CAKE

Cake:

> 1 **white cake mix**
> $^1/_3$ cup **oil**
> 2 **eggs**
> $^1/_2$ cup **water**
> 1 can (21 ounces) **cherry pie filling**

Glaze:

> 1 $^1/_2$ tablespoons **milk**
> 1 cup **powdered sugar**

Preheat oven to 350 degrees.

Mix together cake mix, oil, eggs, and water. Pour batter into greased 9 x 13-inch pan. Stir in pie filling.

Bake 30–35 minutes.

A glaze made from powdered sugar may be drizzled over top, if desired.

LEMON-LIME REFRIGERATOR CAKE

Cake:

1 **lemon cake mix**
1 small package **lime gelatin**

Topping:

1 small box **lemon instant pudding**
8 ounces **whipped topping**

Preheat oven to 350 degrees.

Make cake as directed on box. Bake in a greased 9 x 13-inch pan. Let cool.

Poke deep holes into cake with a fork, spacing them about an inch apart. Dissolve gelatin in 1 cup boiling water. Then add $1/2$ cup cold water to gelatin. Slowly pour gelatin mixture into holes. Refrigerate cake while preparing topping.

In a bowl, mix whipped topping and instant pudding until stiff. Immediately frost cake. Cake must be stored in refrigerator and served chilled.

APPLE PIE-FILLING CAKE

Cake:

1	**white cake mix**
1/3 cup	**oil**
2	**eggs**
1/2 cup	**water**
1 can (21 ounces)	**apple pie filling**

Glaze:

1 tablespoon	**margarine**, melted
1 cup	**powdered sugar**
1/2 teaspoon	**vanilla**
	hot water

Preheat oven to 350 degrees.

Mix together cake mix, oil, eggs, and water. Pour mixture into a greased 9 x 13-inch pan. Marble in apple pie filling.

Bake 30–35 minutes.

Combine margarine, powdered sugar, vanilla, and hot water. Drizzle glaze over cake.

BANANA SPLIT CAKE

$1/4$ teaspoon **baking soda**
$3/4$ cup **buttermilk**
1 **white cake mix**
$1/4$ cup **water**
2 **bananas**, mashed
2 tablespoons **vegetable oil**
3 **egg whites**, whipped
$1/2$ cup **chopped walnuts**
$3/4$ cup **hot-fudge topping**

Preheat oven to 350 degrees.

In a large mixing bowl, dissolve baking soda in buttermilk. Add cake mix, water, bananas, oil, and egg whites.

Spoon half of batter into greased and floured 9 x 13-inch pan. Sprinkle $1/4$ cup walnuts evenly over batter.

Drizzle fudge sauce over walnuts. Top with remaining batter, spreading evenly. Sprinkle remaining walnuts over top.

Bake 30 minutes, or until lightly browned.

PIÑA COLADA CAKE

1 **yellow cake mix**
1 can **crushed pineapple**, drained
1 can (14 ounces) **sweetened condensed milk**
8 ounces **whipped topping**
$^2/_3$ cup **coconut**

Prepare cake mix as directed on the back of package.

Mix $^1/_2$ can of pineapple into batter. Bake according to directions on package.

With a fork, poke holes in warm cake at 1-inch intervals. Pour sweetened condensed milk evenly over cake. Allow cake to cool.

Spread whipped topping over the cake. Sprinkle the top with coconut and remaining pineapple.

CHERRY-CHOCOLATE CAKE

1 **chocolate cake mix**
1 cup **water**
1 **egg**
1 can (21 ounces) **cherry pie filling**

Preheat oven to 350 degrees.

In a large bowl, mix together cake mix, water, and egg until smooth. Fold in cherry pie filling. Pour into a greased 9 x 13-inch pan.

Bake 30—35 minutes, or until cake springs back when touched.

APPLESAUCE CAKE

1 **spice cake mix**
2 cups **applesauce** (16-ounce can)
$^1/_4$ cup **oil**
2 **eggs**
$^1/_4$ cup **wheat germ** (optional)
1 can (16 ounces) **frosting**

Preheat oven to 350 degrees.

Mix together cake mix, applesauce, oil, and eggs in a large bowl. Mix in wheat germ, if desired. Pour mixture into a 9 x 13-inch pan.

Bake 35—40 minutes. Allow cake to cool 10—20 minutes.

Top with frosting of choice. (Cream-cheese frosting is good here.)

FRUIT COCKTAIL CAKE

Cake:

1	**yellow cake mix**
1 small box	**vanilla instant pudding**
1 can	**fruit cocktail with syrup**
3/4 cup	**coconut**
3	**large eggs**
1/4 cup	**oil**
1/2 cup	**light brown sugar**
1/2 cup	**chopped nuts**

Glaze:

1/2 cup	**butter**
1/2 cup	**sugar**
1/2 cup	**evaporated milk**
1 cup	**coconut**
8 ounces	**whipped topping**

Preheat oven to 350 degrees.

In a large bowl, mix together cake mix, pudding mix, fruit cocktail with syrup, coconut, eggs, and oil. Beat with electric mixer 3–5 minutes. Pour into a greased 9 x 13-inch pan. Sprinkle brown sugar and nuts over batter.

Bake 30–35 minutes. Cool 15 minutes.

In a small saucepan, combine butter, sugar, and evaporated milk; boil 2 minutes. Stir in coconut, then pour over cake. Serve warm or cool with whipped topping.

PINEAPPLE-ORANGE CAKE

Cake:

1	**white cake mix**
1 small can	**mandarin oranges with juice**
4	**large eggs**
1/4 cup	**oil**
1/4 cup	**applesauce**

Topping:

8 ounces	**whipped topping**
1 small can	**crushed pineapple with juice**
1 small box	**vanilla instant pudding**

Preheat oven to 350 degrees.

In a large bowl, mix together cake mix, oranges with juice, eggs, oil, and applesauce.

Bake in a greased 9 x 13-inch pan 30 minutes, or until toothpick comes out clean when inserted into center. Chill cake at least 2 hours.

Mix together whipped topping, pineapple with juice, and pudding mix until smooth. Spread on top of cake. Store leftovers in refrigerator.

MANDARIN ORANGE CAKE

Cake:

1	**butter-recipe yellow cake mix**
1/3 cup	**vegetable oil**
3 tablespoons	**water**
3	**large eggs**
1 small can	**mandarin orange slices with juice**

Filling:

12 ounces	**whipped topping**
1 large box	**vanilla instant pudding**
1 can	**crushed pineapple in juice**

Preheat oven to 350 degrees.

Mix together cake mix, oil, water, eggs, and oranges with juice. Place batter into three greased-and-floured round pans.

Bake 23—25 minutes, or until cake springs back when touched.

Mix filling ingredients together by hand and spread between layers and on top and sides of the cake. Keep refrigerated.

PUNCHBOWL CAKE

1 **yellow cake mix**
2 small boxes **vanilla instant pudding**
1 can **crushed pineapple**, drained
1 can (21 ounces) **cherry pie filling**
12 ounces **whipped topping**
1/2 cup **chopped nuts**

Prepare cake and pudding according to package directions. Crumble one half of cake into bottom of punchbowl. Pour half the pudding over cake. Crumble the other half of cake into the bowl and pour rest of pudding over that layer. Add pineapple, then cherry pie filling, then topping. Sprinkle nuts on top. Serve immediately. Refrigerate any leftovers.

TROPICAL GETAWAY CAKE

Cake:

1	**yellow cake mix**
3	**eggs**
1/2 cup	**vegetable oil**
1/2 cup	**applesauce**
1 small can	**mandarin oranges**, drained

Glaze:

1 cup	**crushed pineapple with juice**
3 tablespoons	**cornstarch**
1 cup	**sugar**

Topping:

4	**bananas**, sliced
1 cup	**1-percent milk**
1 small box	**vanilla instant pudding**
8 ounces	**whipped topping**
1/3 cup	**coconut**

Preheat oven to 350 degrees.

Mix together cake mix, eggs, oil, applesauce, and oranges until smooth, then pour into a greased 9 x 13-inch pan.

Bake 30–35 minutes, or until golden brown. Allow cake to cool.

Prepare glaze by mixing pineapple with juice, cornstarch, and sugar in a small saucepan. Cook over medium heat, stirring constantly until thick and clear. Pour over cake.

Right before serving, place sliced bananas on top of pineapple layer. Blend pudding mix and milk with wire whisk. Fold in whipped topping. Spread over cake. Sprinkle coconut over top.

PEACH CAKE

1 **white cake mix**
1 can (21 ounces) **peach pie filling**
3 **eggs**
$^{1}/_{2}$ cup **sour cream**
1 package (8 ounces) **cream cheese,** softened
1 small box **vanilla instant pudding**
1 can (16 ounces) **crushed pineapple with juice**
8 ounces **whipped topping**

With fork, mix together cake mix, pie filling, and eggs. Gently add sour cream. Spread batter into a greased 9 x 13-inch glass pan.

Bake 30—35 minutes. Cool completely.

Mix together cream cheese, instant pudding, and crushed pineapple with juice. Gently fold whipped topping into cream cheese mixture. Spread onto cool cake. Keep refrigerated until ready to serve. Refrigerate leftovers.

APPLE-SPICE CAKE

          1 **spice cake mix**
    3 small **apples**
1 can (14 ounces) **sweetened condensed milk**
          1 cup **sour cream**
        ¹/₄ cup **lemon juice**
    1 teaspoon **ground cinnamon**

Preheat oven to 350 degrees.

Prepare cake mix batter according to the package directions. Peel, slice, core, and cut apples into small pieces. Stir apples into batter, then pour into a greased 9 x 13-inch pan.

Bake 28—30 minutes, or until toothpick inserted into center comes out clean.

Combine sweetened condensed milk, sour cream, and lemon juice.

Take cake from oven and spread sour cream mixture over top of cake. Return to oven; bake 8—10 minutes longer, or until done. Sprinkle cinnamon over the top. Cool. Refrigerate leftovers.

HAWAIIAN PINEAPPLE CAKE

1 **yellow cake mix**
8 ounces **cream cheese**, softened
1 large box **vanilla instant pudding**
1 can (16 ounces) **pineapple chunks**, drained
12 ounces **whipped topping**
$^{1}/_{3}$ cup **coconut**

Make cake mix according to directions on back and bake in a 9 x 13-inch pan. Cool.

Make pudding according to box directions and set aside. Mix softened cream cheese with prepared pudding until smooth. Pour mixture onto cake.

Sprinkle pineapple chunks over pudding mixture, and then smooth on whipped topping. Sprinkle with coconut. Refrigerate.

PINEAPPLE-CHERRY DUMP CAKE

1 **yellow cake mix**
¹/₂ to 1 stick **butter** or **margarine**, thinly sliced
1 can (20 ounces) **crushed pineapple with juice**
1 can (21 ounces) **cherry pie filling**

Preheat oven to 350 degrees.

Grease a 9 x 13-inch pan. Dump in half the cake mix and spread evenly. Dump pineapple with juice over cake mix and spread evenly. Spread pie filling over pineapple. Dump rest of cake mix evenly over the top. Put butter slices over the top.

Bake 48–53 minutes.

Serve warm with vanilla ice cream or chilled with whipped topping.

APPLE STREUSEL

Batter:

> 1 **yellow cake mix**
> 2 **large eggs**
> ¹/₂ teaspoon **lemon extract**
> 1 can (21 ounces) **apple pie filling**

Topping:

> ¹/₄ cup **butter** or **margarine**, melted
> ¹/₂ cup **sugar**
> ¹/₂ cup **flour**
> ¹/₂ teaspoon **cinnamon**

Preheat oven to 350 degrees.

Mix together cake mix, eggs, lemon extract, and apple pie filling. Pour batter into a greased 9 x 13-inch baking dish.

Prepare topping with melted butter, sugar, flour, and cinnamon. Mix with a fork until crumbly. Sprinkle mixture over top of batter.

Bake 42–47 minutes.

CHERRY COFFEE CAKE

Cake:

1 **yellow cake mix**, divided
1 cup **all-purpose flour**
1 package **active dry yeast**
²/₃ cup **warm water**
2 **large eggs**
1 can (21 ounces) **cherry pie filling**
¹/₃ cup **butter** or **margarine**

Glaze:

1 cup **sifted powdered sugar**
2 tablespoons **water**

Preheat oven to 350 degrees.

Mix together 1¹/₂ cups cake mix, flour, and yeast in a bowl. Add warm water, stirring until smooth. Stir in eggs. Spread batter evenly into a greased 9 x 13-inch pan. Spoon pie filling evenly over batter.

In a separate bowl, cut butter into remaining cake mix with fork until crumbly. Sprinkle mixture over pie filling.

Bake 25–30 minutes. Allow cake to cool.

Combine powdered sugar and water. Drizzle over cake. Cut cake into squares.

BLUEBERRY DUMP CAKE

1 **yellow cake mix**, divided
1 can (20 ounces) **crushed pineapple with juice**
1 can (21 ounces) **blueberry pie filling**
1 stick **margarine**

Preheat oven to 350 degrees.

Grease a 9 x 13-inch pan. Sprinkle half of cake mix over bottom of pan. Pour crushed pineapple with juice over cake mix. Spread blueberry pie filling over top of pineapple. Sprinkle remaining half of cake mix over the top. With a sharp knife, cut the margarine into small strips and place evenly over the top of cake.

Bake 45–50 minutes.

VALENTINE LOVE CAKE

1	**French Vanilla cake mix**
1 large carton	**frozen sweetened strawberries**
1 small package	**French Vanilla** or **cheesecake instant pudding**
2 cups	**milk**
8 ounces	**whipped topping**, thawed
	fresh strawberries, for decorating top

Preheat oven to 350 degrees.

Prepare and bake cake according to instructions on box. Allow cake to cool, and then refrigerate several hours.

Immediately before serving, poke holes at 1-inch intervals over top of cake using a wooden spoon handle. Spoon strawberries and juice evenly over top of cake, allowing mixture to soak into holes.

For topping, mix together pudding mix and milk. Spread over strawberry layer. Spread whipped topping over pudding. Slice fresh strawberries and arrange on top of cake in the shape of a heart.

FANCY CAKES

DUMP CAKE

1 **yellow cake mix**
1 can (29 ounces) **sliced peaches** with juice
$^1/_2$ to 1 stick **butter** or **margarine**, thinly sliced

Preheat oven to 350 degrees.

Grease a 9 x 13-inch pan. Spread half of cake mix evenly in bottom of pan. Pour can of sliced peaches and juice evenly over the cake mix. Cover the peaches with the rest of the cake mix, then slice the margarine on top.

Bake 50 minutes, or until golden brown.

STRAWBERRY-BANANA GELATIN POKE CAKE

1 **white cake mix**
1 small package **strawberry-banana flavored gelatin**
1 cup **boiling water**
$^1/_2$ cup **cold water**
8 ounces **whipped topping**

Bake cake according to directions on box. Allow cake to cool. With a fork, poke holes in the cake, thoroughly covering it.

Stir gelatin mix with boiling water until mix is dissolved. Then, add $^1/_2$ cup cold water to hot gelatin water. Pour over cake. Chill 4 hours.

Top with whipped topping before serving. Store leftovers in refrigerator.

STRAWBERRY DECADENCE

1 **French Vanilla**
or **strawberry cake mix**
2 bags (10 ounces each) **frozen sliced strawberries**,
thawed and sweetened
1 small box **French Vanilla** or
cheesecake-flavored
instant pudding
8 ounces **whipped topping**

Bake cake in a greased 9 x 13-inch pan according to directions on box. Cool, then poke holes in cake (the handle of a wooden spoon works well).

Pour the strawberries and juice over the cake so the berries and juice seep into the holes. Spread strawberries around until the cake is covered.

After preparing the pudding according to directions on box, smooth it over the berries, sealing them. Ice the cake with the whipped topping and enjoy! Keep refrigerated for best flavor.

YOGURT CAKE

Cake:

> 1 **white cake mix**
> 8 ounces **flavored yogurt** (blueberry and boysenberry
> are good choices)

Topping:

> 8 ounces **whipped topping**
> 8 ounces **flavored yogurt** (same flavor as used in cake)

Preheat oven to 350 degrees.

With electric mixer, slowly mix cake ingredients according to package directions. Gently stir in yogurt with spoon or plastic spatula. Pour batter into a greased 9 x 13-inch pan.

Bake 30–35 minutes, until golden on top. Use a toothpick to determine if cake is done. Chill the cake in the refrigerator 4 hours.

Before serving, stir whipped topping and yogurt together and frost cake with it. Store leftovers in the refrigerator.

COOKIES-AND-CREAM CAKE

Cake:

> 1 **white cake mix**
> 1 1/4 cups **water**
> 1/3 cup **vegetable oil**
> 3 **egg whites**
> 1 1/2 cups **Oreo cookies,** crushed

Frosting:

> 1 can (16 ounces) **vanilla frosting**
> 1/2 cups **Oreo cookies,** crushed

Preheat oven to 350 degrees.

In large bowl, combine cake mix, water, oil, and egg whites until smooth; gently stir in crushed cookies. Pour batter into greased-and-floured 9 x 13-inch pan.

Bake 25–35 minutes, or until toothpick inserted in center comes out clean. Cool completely.

Mix frosting ingredients and spread over cake.

HEATH BAR CAKE

1 **chocolate cake mix**
1 can (14 ounces) **sweetened condensed milk**
1 small jar **butterscotch topping**
12 ounces **whipped topping**
4 small **Heath** (or **Skor**) **bars**, chopped

Prepare cake according to directions on package, and bake in a 9 x 13-inch pan.

While still hot, use a wooden spoon handle to poke holes in the top of the cake. Pour condensed milk evenly over the top, then pour butterscotch topping evenly over that. Sprinkle half of chopped Heath bars over the top. Refrigerate at least 3 hours.

Spread whipped topping over cake, then sprinkle with remaining Heath pieces.

BUTTERFINGER CAKE

1 **German Chocolate cake mix**
8 or 12 ounces **butterscotch topping**
4 small **Butterfinger bars**
12 ounces **whipped topping**
$^1/_2$ cup **chopped nuts** (pecans are good here)

Prepare cake batter according to instructions on the box. Bake cake in a 9 x 13-inch pan.

While cake is still hot, poke small holes in cake. Pour butterscotch topping over cake so that topping can soak in. Cool completely.

Crush Butterfinger bars. Reserve one bar and mix the rest into whipped topping along with the nuts. Spread over cooled cake and sprinkle with remaining Butterfinger crumbs. Refrigerate until ready to serve.

PUDDING POKE CAKE

1 **white cake mix**
4 cups **2-percent milk**
2 small boxes **lemon instant pudding**

Prepare and bake cake mix as directed on package in a 9 x 13-inch pan. Remove from oven. Immediately poke holes at 1-inch intervals clear through cake with round handle of a wooden spoon.

Add milk to the pudding mix and beat with wire whisk 2 minutes. Quickly pour half the thin pudding mixture evenly over warm cake and into holes to make stripes. Refrigerate remaining pudding mixture until slightly thick. Spoon over top of cake, swirling to frost cake.

Refrigerate at least 1 hour. Store leftover cake in refrigerator.

Other Flavor Combinations:

Cake Mix:	Pudding Mix (use any one):
Lemon	Lemon
White	Butterscotch
	Chocolate
	Pistachio
	Vanilla
Chocolate	Chocolate
	Pistachio
	Vanilla
	Banana Cream
	Coconut Cream
Yellow	Butterscotch
	Chocolate
	Pistachio

CHERRY CHUNK CAKE

1 **chocolate cake mix**
2 **eggs**
1 can (21 ounces) **cherry pie filling**
$^3/_4$ cup **chopped nuts**
$^3/_4$ cup **chocolate chips**
$^1/_2$ cup **brown sugar**

Preheat oven to 350 degrees.

Mix together cake mix, eggs, and pie filling. Put into a greased 9 x 13-inch pan. Sprinkle nuts, chocolate chips, and brown sugar on top.

Bake 30–35 minutes.

CONFETTI CAKE

Cake:

1	**yellow cake mix**
1 small box	**vanilla instant pudding**
3	**large eggs**
1 cup	**water**
$1/4$ cup	**vegetable oil**
$1/4$ cup	**applesauce**
$3/4$ cup	**semisweet chocolate chips**

Topping:

1 cup	**colored mini-marshmallows**
1 container	**chocolate frosting**
$1/4$ cup	**semisweet chocolate chips**

Preheat oven to 350 degrees.

In a large bowl, mix together cake mix, pudding mix, eggs, water, oil, and applesauce until smooth. Stir in chocolate chips. Pour into greased and floured 9 x 13-inch pan.

Bake 40—45 minutes, or until toothpick inserted into center comes out clean.

Immediately arrange marshmallows evenly over hot cake. Place frosting in microwave-safe bowl. Microwave on HIGH 25—30 seconds. Stir until smooth, then drizzle evenly over marshmallows and cake. Sprinkle with chocolate chips. Cool completely.

CHOCOLATE-LOVER'S CAKE

1 **devil's food cake mix**
1 small box **chocolate instant pudding**
1 can (12 ounces) **lemon-lime soda**
1/3 cup **vegetable oil**
4 **eggs**
1 container **chocolate frosting**

Preheat oven to 350 degrees.

In large bowl, combine cake mix, pudding, soda, oil, and eggs with electric mixer. Pour batter evenly into a greased 9 x 13-inch pan.

Bake 30 to 35 minutes. Cool and frost with frosting of choice.

EASY CHEESECAKE

Bottom Layer:

1 **yellow cake mix**

Filling:

2 packages (8 ounces each) **cream cheese**, softened
1/2 cup **sugar**
3/4 teaspoon **vanilla**
2 **eggs**
1/4 cup **sour cream**

Topping:

2 squares **unsweetened chocolate**
3 tablespoons **margarine**
2 tablespoons **boiling water**
1 cup **powdered sugar**
3/4 teaspoon **vanilla**

Bottom Layer:

Heat oven to 350 degrees.

Grease bottom of a 9-inch springform pan. Prepare cake mix as directed on package; pour half of the batter evenly into greased springform pan. (Suggestion: use extra batter to make a plain cake in a small round pan.)

Bake 20 minutes.

Filling:

Beat cream cheese, sugar, and vanilla with electric mixer until well blended. Add eggs one at a time, mixing at low speed after each addition just until blended. Add in sour cream; pour cream-cheese mixture over cake.

Bake 35 minutes, or until center is almost set. Run knife around rim of pan to separate cake from side of pan.

Topping:

Melt chocolate and margarine over low heat, stirring until smooth. Remove from heat. Add water, sugar, and vanilla; mix well. Spread over cooled cheesecake. Refrigerate at least 4 hours or overnight.

ORANGE-PUMPKIN CAKE

Cake:

1	**yellow cake mix**
3	**egg whites**
1 1/4 cup	**canned pumpkin**
1 cup	**orange juice**
1/3 cup	**sour cream**
1 1/2 teaspoons	**vanilla**
1 teaspoon	**cinnamon**
1/2 teaspoon	**nutmeg**
1/2 teaspoon	**allspice**

Glaze:

1 1/2 cups	**powdered sugar**
1/4 teaspoon	**vanilla**
	water

Preheat oven to 350 degrees.

Mix together all the cake ingredients together 2–3 minutes. Pour into a greased-and-floured bundt pan.

Bake 35–40 minutes. While hot, invert cake onto serving platter.

Mix powdered sugar and vanilla, and gradually add water a tablespoon at a time until it reaches desired consistency; drizzle over cake. Cool.

BUTTERFINGER CRUMB CAKE

1	**chocolate cake mix**
2 small boxes	**vanilla instant pudding**
4 cups	**milk**
2 large	**Butterfinger candy bars**, chopped
12 ounces	**whipped topping**

Prepare and bake cake according to instructions on box in a greased 9 x 13-inch pan. Allow cake to cool, then crumble into bowl.

Mix instant pudding with milk until set. Pour half the pudding in the bottom of a large glass bowl. Sprinkle half the cake crumbs over pudding. Pat cake into pudding. Sprinkle $1/3$ Butterfinger crumbs over pudding and cake crumbs. Layer remaining pudding, then press the rest of cake crumbs into pudding. Sprinkle $1/3$ Butterfinger crumbs over cake. Spread whipped topping over cake. Sprinkle remaining Butterfinger crumbs over whipped topping.

SWISS-CHOCOLATE DUMP CAKE

1 **Swiss chocolate cake mix**
1 can (20 ounces) **crushed pineapple with juice**
1 can (21 ounces) **cherry pie filling**
3/4 cup **chopped pecans**
1/2 cup **butter** or **margarine**

Preheat oven to 350 degrees.

Dump half the cake mix into a greased 9 x 13-inch pan. Dump pineapple with juice evenly over mix. Dump pie filling evenly over pineapple. Sprinkle remaining cake mix evenly over cherry layer. Sprinkle pecans over cake mix. Melt butter and drizzle over top.

Bake 45–50 minutes, or until set. Serve warm or at room temperature.

CHOCOLATE-CRUMB PUDDING CAKE

1 **chocolate cake mix**
3/4 cup **semisweet chocolate chips**
1 small box **French Vanilla instant pudding**
1 cup **chocolate** (or **caramel**) **sauce**
1 package (12 ounces) **whipped topping**, thawed
1/2 cup **chopped nuts**

Prepare cake according to instructions on the box. Add the chocolate chips to the batter.

Bake in a greased 9 x 13-inch pan. Allow cake to cool, then crumble it.

Make pudding according to package directions and allow to set in refrigerator 5 minutes. Then spread into bottom of a 9 x 13-inch pan or a large glass bowl. Sprinkle half the cake crumbs over top of pudding and gently press into pudding. Drizzle 3/4 cup of the chocolate sauce over the crumbs. Add remaining cake crumbs, gently pressing into cake pan or bowl. Spread whipped topping over cake. Refrigerate until ready to serve.

Just before serving, drizzle with remaining chocolate sauce and sprinkle with chopped nuts.

UPSIDE-DOWN GERMAN CHOCOLATE CAKE

1	**German Chocolate cake mix**
1 cup	**coconut**
1 cup	**chopped nuts**
$^1/_2$ cup	**chocolate chips**
$^3/_4$ cup	**butter** or **margarine**
8 ounces	**cream cheese**, softened
1 box (1 pound)	**confectioner's sugar**

Preheat oven to 350 degrees.

Mix together coconut and nuts. Put in the bottom of a greased 9 x 13-inch pan. Sprinkle chocolate chips over the coconut and nuts.

Mix cake mix according to directions on the box and pour over bottom layer.

In a separate bowl, beat together butter and cream cheese with an electric mixture. Slowly add in powdered sugar, mixing well. Pour over cake batter.

Bake 40—50 minutes

LEMONADE CAKE

1 **lemon cake mix**
1 cup **frozen lemonade concentrate**, thawed
1 cup **powdered sugar**
1 container **lemon** or **vanilla frosting**

Heat oven to 350 degrees.

Prepare and bake cake as directed on package in greased 9 x 13-inch pan. Cool 15 minutes.

Stir together lemonade concentrate and powdered sugar. Poke holes in warm cake with fork. Drizzle lemonade mixture evenly over cake. Refrigerate cake until cold.

Spread frosting over cold cake. Cover and refrigerate leftover cake.

CHOCONUT CAKE

Cake:

1	**dark-chocolate cake mix**
1 cup	**milk**
1 cup	**sugar**
24 large	**marshmallows**
1 $^1/_2$ cups	**coconut**

Topping:

1 $^1/_2$ cups	**sugar**
$^1/_2$ cup	**evaporated milk**
$^1/_2$ cup	**butter** or **margarine**
1 $^1/_2$ cups	**chocolate chips**

Prepare cake mix as directed on the back of box. Pour batter onto a large sheet-cake pan, but bake for regular allotted time specified on box for cake pans.

Mix together milk, sugar, and marshmallows in a saucepan. Heat until marshmallows are melted. Remove from heat and add coconut. Spread marshmallow mixture over warm cake.

In a different saucepan, combine all topping ingredients except chocolate chips, and cook until boiling. Take off heat and add chocolate chips, stirring until chips are melted. Spread on top of cake.

CHOCOLATE CARAMEL CAKE

1 **German chocolate cake mix**
1 jar **caramel ice cream topping**
1 cup **chocolate chips**
$^3/_4$ cup **chopped nuts**

Bake cake as directed on box in a 9 x 13-inch pan.

While still hot, pour caramel ice cream topping over cake. Sprinkle caramel layer with chocolate chips and chopped nuts. Can serve cooled or while still warm.

MARBLED LOVE CAKE

1 **fudge marble cake mix**
3/4 cup **butter** or **margarine**
8 ounces **cream cheese**, softened
1 box (1 pound) **powdered sugar**

Preheat oven to 350 degrees.

Mix cake as directed on box. Pour into greased and floured
9 x 13-inch pan.

In separate bowl, combine butter, cream cheese, and powdered
sugar; mix well. Spoon over top of cake batter.

Bake 45—50 minutes. Cool. Refrigerate leftovers.

CARAMEL-PECAN CHOCOLATE CAKE

1 **chocolate cake mix**
1 can (14 ounces) **sweetened condensed milk**
1 small jar **caramel ice cream topping**
12 ounces **whipped topping**
3/4 cup **chopped pecans**, divided

Preheat oven to 350 degrees.

Prepare cake according to directions on the box. Pour batter into a greased 9 x 13-inch pan.

Bake 30–35 minutes. Let cake cool about 30 minutes.

Poke holes in cake with the handle of a wooden spoon. Pour can of condensed milk evenly over cake. Pour jar of caramel ice cream topping over condensed-milk layer. Sprinkle 1/2 cup pecans over cake. Refrigerate 2 to 3 hours.

Before serving, spread whipped topping over cake. Sprinkle remaining pecans over whipped topping.

GELATIN POKE CAKE

1 **white cake mix**
1 small package **gelatin**, any flavor
1 cup **boiling water**
$1/2$ cup **cold water**
8 ounces **whipped topping**

Prepare and bake white cake as directed on box. Allow cake to cool.

Poke holes in cake with a fork. Dissolve gelatin in 1 cup boiling water, then mix in $1/2$ cup cold water. Pour gelatin mixture over cake. Chill 4 hours. Garnish with whipped topping.

Bunot Cakes

LEMON POPPY-SEED CAKE

Cake:

1	**lemon cake mix**
1 small box	**lemon instant pudding**
2 tablespoons	**poppy seeds**
4	**eggs**
1/4 cup	**vegetable oil**
1/4 cup	**applesauce**
1 cup	**water**

Glaze:

1/3 cup	**lemon juice**
1 1/3 cups	**powdered sugar**

Preheat oven to 350 degrees.

In a large bowl, mix all cake ingredients together until smooth. Pour batter into a greased and floured bundt pan and bake 50 minutes.

Invert hot cake onto a platter. Mix lemon juice with powdered sugar. Pierce the top of the cake generously with a fork and pour icing onto hot cake. Allow icing to soak into cake 5 minutes. Ready to serve.

DEATH-BY-CHOCOLATE CAKE

³/4 cup **sour cream**
4 **eggs**
¹/2 cup **water**
¹/2 cup **oil**
1 **chocolate cake mix**
1 small box **instant chocolate pudding**
1 cup **semisweet chocolate chips**
powdered sugar

Preheat oven to 350 degrees.

Beat sour cream, eggs, water, and oil together in a large bowl until thoroughly mixed. Add cake mix and pudding mix. Stir in chocolate chips. Place batter in a greased and floured bundt pan.

Bake 45–55 minutes, or until a fork inserted into cake comes out clean.

While still hot, invert cake onto a serving platter. When cool, sift powdered sugar over top of cake.

BANANA BUNDT CAKE

2 **bananas**, mashed
1 **white cake mix**
1 small box **vanilla instant pudding**
3 **eggs**
1 cup **sour cream**
$^1/_3$ cup **water**
2 tablespoons **oil**
$^1/_4$ teaspoon **baking powder**
1 can (16 ounces) **white frosting**

Preheat oven to 350 degrees.

Combine bananas, cake mix, pudding, eggs, sour cream, water, oil, and baking powder. Mix just until moistened. Pour batter into greased and floured bundt pan.

Bake 45–50 minutes. Invert cake onto a platter and let cool.

Place frosting in microwave 10-15 seconds to soften. Drizzle over cake.

PISTACHIO CAKE

1	**yellow cake mix**
3	**large eggs**
1 cup	**club soda**
2 small boxes	**pistachio instant pudding**
1/3 cup	**vegetable oil**
1 1/4 cups	**finely chopped white pistachio nuts** or **pecans**, divided
12 ounces	**whipped topping**

Preheat oven to 350 degrees.

In a large bowl, combine cake mix, eggs, club soda, 1 box of pudding, oil, and 1/2 cup nuts. Mix well and pour into a greased and floured bundt or tube cake pan.

Bake 40–50 minutes. Cake is done when a long toothpick inserted into middle of cake comes out clean. Invert cake onto the cooling rack and remove pan to cool completely. When cool, place cake on serving plate.

To make icing, mix carton of whipped topping with remaining box of pudding. Spread evenly over cake. Sprinkle with remaining nuts.

PISTACHIO POUND CAKE

1	**white cake mix**
1 small box	**pistachio instant pudding**
1/2 cup	**orange juice**
1/2 cup	**oil**
1/2 cup	**water**
3 large	**eggs**
4 drops	**green food coloring**
1/2 cup	**chocolate syrup**

Preheat oven to 350 degrees.

In a large bowl, mix together cake mix, pudding mix, orange juice, oil, and water. Add eggs one at a time, mixing well after each. Add food coloring.

Set aside 1 1/2 cups of batter. Pour rest of batter into bundt pan. Mix chocolate syrup into reserved batter. Pour over top of cake in tube pan.

Bake 50 minutes, or until a toothpick inserted into cake comes out clean.

INCREDIBLE BUNDT CAKE

1 **butter-recipe yellow cake mix**
1 small box **vanilla instant pudding**
1 cup **sour cream**
3 **large eggs**
$^1/_4$ cup **vegetable oil**
$^1/_4$ cup **applesauce**
1 cup **semisweet chocolate chips**, divided
1 cup **chopped pecans**, divided

Preheat oven to 350 degrees.

Using an electric mixer, blend cake mix, pudding, sour cream, eggs, oil, and applesauce 5–6 minutes. Grease and flour a bundt or tube pan. Pour $^1/_3$ of the batter into pan and sprinkle half the chocolate chips and pecans over it. Pour in remaining batter and top with remaining chips and nuts.

Bake 50 to 55 minutes. Cool about 5 minutes, then turn out onto a serving plate; cool completely.

CREAM CHEESE-
LEMON POUND CAKE

8 ounces	**cream cheese**
3	**large eggs**
1	**yellow cake mix**
1 small box	**lemon** or **vanilla instant pudding**
3/4 cup	**milk**
1/2 teaspoon	**lemon extract**
2 tablespoons	**lemon zest**

Preheat oven to 350 degrees.

In a large bowl, beat cream cheese at medium speed with electric mixer until smooth and fluffy. Add eggs one at a time, beating well after each egg. In a separate bowl, mix together cake mix and pudding.

In two or three intervals, add pudding/cake-mix powder alternately with milk into the cream-cheese mixture. Beat just until smooth. Gently stir in the lemon extract and zest. Pour batter into greased and floured bundt pan.

Bake 50 minutes.

LUSCIOUS LEMON CAKE

Cake:

I	**yellow cake mix**
I small box	**lemon** or **vanilla instant pudding**
I teaspoon	**lemon extract**
3/4 cup	**water**
1/2 cup	**vegetable oil**
1/4 cup	**applesauce**
4	**eggs**

Icing:

I cup	**powdered sugar**
1/3 cup	**orange juice**

Preheat oven to 350 degrees.

In a large bowl, mix together cake mix, pudding mix, lemon extract, water, oil, and applesauce. Beat until smooth. Add eggs one at a time, beating well after each addition. Beat on high 8 minutes. Pour batter into a greased tube or bundt pan.

Bake 50 minutes, or until toothpick inserted into center of cake comes out clean. Invert hot cake onto a serving platter.

Combine powdered sugar and orange juice. Drizzle glaze over cake.

Muffins
and
Bread

OATMEAL-RAISIN MUFFINS

1 **yellow cake mix**
1 1/3 cups **water**
1/3 cup **vegetable oil**
2 **large eggs**
2 cups **quick oats**
1 cup **raisins**
1/2 cup **chopped nuts**
1 1/2 teaspoons **cinnamon**

Preheat oven to 350 degrees.

Grease and flour muffin pan or use paper muffin cups. Mix together cake mix, water, oil, eggs, and quick oats in large bowl until well blended. Stir in raisins, nuts, and cinnamon. Fill muffin cups 3/4 full with batter.

Bake 20–25 minutes.

EASY BANANA BREAD

            2 medium **bananas**, mashed
                  1   **banana cake mix**
        1 small box **banana instant pudding**
                  3   **eggs**
            $1/4$ cup **vegetable oil**
            $1/4$ cup **applesauce**
       $3/4$ teaspoon **ground cinnamon**
            $1/2$ cup **water**
            $3/4$ cup **finely chopped nuts**

Preheat oven to 350 degrees.

Blend all ingredients together until smooth. Fill greased bread pans $3/4$ full.

Bake about 30 minutes or until a toothpick inserted into top of bread comes out clean.

BANANA-NUT MUFFINS

                  1   **banana** or **spice cake mix**
                  2   **eggs**
              1 cup **water**
            $1/3$ cup **chopped nuts**
            $1/3$ cup **vegetable oil**
          1 medium **banana**, mashed

Preheat oven to 350 degrees.

Grease and flour muffin pan or use paper muffin cups. Mix together cake mix. eggs, water, nuts, oil, and banana in a large bowl until well blended. Fill muffin cups $3/4$ full with batter.

Bake 20–25 minutes.

CHOCOLATE-CHOCOLATE CHIP MUFFINS

I	**chocolate-fudge cake mix**
I small box	**chocolate instant pudding**
$^3/_4$ cup	**water**
3	**eggs,** beaten
$^1/_4$ cup	**applesauce**
$^1/_4$ cup	**vegetable oil**
$^1/_4$ teaspoon	**almond extract**
$^3/_4$ cup	**chocolate chips,** frozen

Preheat oven to 350 degrees.

Grease and flour muffin pan or use paper muffin cups. Mix together cake mix, pudding, water, eggs, applesauce, oil, and almond extract until smooth. Stir in chocolate chips last. Fill cups $^3/_4$ full.

Bake about 23–33 minutes, or until done when tested with a toothpick.

QUICK AND EASY CORNBREAD

1 small box **cornbread mix**
1 **yellow cake mix**

Preheat oven to 350 degrees.

Mix boxes together according to directions on back of each box.
Pour batter into a greased 9 x 13-inch pan.

Bake approximately 25–35 minutes, or until done.

CHILDREN'S
DELIGHTS

QUICK AND EASY APPLE CRISP

4–6 **apples** (about 6 cups)
1 **yellow cake mix**
1/2 cup **quick oats**
2 tablespoons **sugar**
1 tablespoon **cinnamon**
1/2 cup **butter** or **margarine**, melted

Preheat oven to 350 degrees.

Peel, core, and slice apples. Spread over the bottom of a greased 8 x 8-inch pan.

Mix cake mix, oats, sugar, and cinnamon together in large bowl. Pour melted butter over the top. Mix with fork until crumbly.

Bake 35–40 minutes, until apples are tender and top is golden brown.

SNICKERS SURPRISE COOKIES

1 **yellow** or **chocolate cake mix**
2 **eggs**
$^1/_3$ cup **vegetable oil**
1 bag snack-size **Snickers bars**

Heat oven to 350 degrees.

Mix together cake mix, eggs, and oil in a bowl until all the cake powder is absorbed.

Cut small Snickers bars in half. Place a half in the center of a ball of dough. Make sure the candy bar is completely covered with dough.

Bake cookies 8–10 minutes, or until done.

DELICIOUS DIRT

1	**devil's food cake mix**
8 ounces	**cream cheese,** softened
$^1/_4$ cup	**margarine** or **butter,** softened
3 $^1/_2$ cups	**1-percent milk**
2 small boxes	**chocolate instant pudding**
8 ounces	**whipped topping**
$^1/_2$ package	**Oreo cookies,** crushed

Prepare and bake cake according to directions on package box, then cool. Crumble cake into a large bowl.

In a clean bowl, mix together cream cheese and margarine with an electric mixer. Add milk and pudding mix, blending until thickened. Gently fold the whipped topping into the pudding mixture. Spoon the pudding mixture on top of cake crumbs. Crush cookies and place them on top of pudding mixture. Refrigerate leftovers.

ICE CREAM-CONE CUPCAKES

1 **chocolate cake mix**
1 1/4 cups **water**
1/4 cup **vegetable oil**
1/4 cup **applesauce**
2 **large eggs**
30 **flat-bottom ice cream cones**
1 can (16 ounces) **frosting** (any flavor)
candy sprinkles (optional)

Preheat oven to 350 degrees.

In large bowl, mix together cake mix, water, oil, applesauce, and eggs until smooth. Fill each cone with about 2 1/2 tablespoons of batter. Place upright cones about 3 inches apart on an ungreased baking sheet or muffin pan.

Bake approximately 25–30 minutes. Cool completely.

Soften frosting in the microwave on HIGH 10 seconds. Stir, then spread evenly over cupcakes. Place candy sprinkles on top, if desired.

EASY
ICE CREAM SANDWICHES

1 **devil's food cake mix**
1/3 cup **oil**
2 **eggs**
1/2 gallon **vanilla ice cream**

Preheat oven to 350 degrees.

Mix together cake mix, oil, and eggs in a large bowl. The dough will be stiff.

Lightly flour a clean surface. Roll out the dough with a rolling pin until it is about 1/2-inch thick. Use a round cup or cookie cutter to cut out uniform cookies. Spray a cookie sheet with vegetable oil. Place the cut-out dough on the pan.

Bake 8–10 minutes. Remove cookies onto a cooling rack.

When cool, place a scoopful of ice cream in-between two cookies. Wrap the sandwiches in plastic wrap. Store cookies in an airtight container in the freezer.

VALENTINE COOKIES

1	**cherry-chip cake mix**
2	**eggs**
1/3 cup	**vegetable oil**
1 can (16 ounces)	**white frosting**
	red food coloring

Preheat oven to 350 degrees.

Mix together cake mix, eggs, and oil in a large bowl until dough is formed. Scoop round balls of dough onto greased cookie sheet. Form each ball into the shape of a heart.

Bake 8–12 minutes, or until slightly golden brown.

Frost with white frosting mixed with a little red food coloring. Place sprinkles on top, if desired.

AMERICAN FLAG CAKE

1 **white cake mix**
1 small box **strawberry gelatin**
1 cup **boiling water**
$^1/_2$ cup **cold water**
2 cups **whipped topping**
1 $^1/_2$ cups **strawberries**, sliced
$^1/_2$ cup **blueberries**
2 **bananas**, sliced

Prepare cake following package directions and bake in 9 x 13-inch pan. Poke cake at 1-inch intervals with a fork.

Dissolve gelatin in boiling water, then stir in cold water. Slowly drizzle gelatin over cake. Chill 3 hours. Spread with whipped topping. To resemble a flag, arrange strawberries and bananas as stripes and blueberries as stars on cake.

JACK-O-LANTERN CAKE

2 **cake mixes**, any flavor
2 cans **white frosting**
   food coloring
1 **Hostess Ho-Ho** (or similar cake-roll snack item)

Prepare two cakes in greased and floured bundt pans; remove from pans and cool completely.

Color most of the frosting a deep orange, reserving about $1/2$ cup. Color this amount black or use dark-chocolate fudge frosting.

Place one bundt cake upside down (rounded side on the bottom) on cake plate; frost top only. Place second bundt cake flat-side down on top of first cake. Frost entire cake with orange frosting, making up-and-down motions with spatula to simulate pumpkin curves. Insert Ho-Ho in the middle of top bundt cake to make the stem. Use black frosting to make eyes, nose, mouth, etc. Black rope licorice may also be used.

BLACK CAT COOKIES

³/₄ cup **crunchy peanut butter**
2 **eggs**
¹/₃ cup **water**
1 **chocolate cake mix**
plain M&Ms
Red Hots

Heat oven to 350 degrees.

Beat together peanut butter, eggs, and water. Gradually add cake mix and blend well. Form dough into 1-inch balls. Place on lightly greased cookie sheet and flatten balls with bottom of a glass dipped in sugar. Pinch out 2 ears at top of cookie. Add M&Ms as eyes and a Red Hot as a nose. Press fork into the sides of the cat face to form whiskers.

Bake 8–10 minutes.

PUMPKIN-PATCH HALLOWEEN CAKE

Cake:

I	**yellow cake mix**
$3/4$ cup	**unsalted roasted peanuts**, chopped
I cup	**water**
$1/3$ cup	**oil**
2	**eggs**

Topping:

I can (16 ounces)	**vanilla frosting**
$1/3$ cup	**peanut butter**
$1/2$ cup	**unsalted roasted peanuts**, chopped
I small	**Butterfinger bar**, chopped
16	**candy pumpkins**

Preheat oven to 350 degrees.

Grease and flour a 9 x 13-inch pan. In a large bowl, combine all cake ingredients. Mix with electric mixer on slow speed until there is no powder visible. Pour into prepared pan.

Bake 30–40 minutes, or until toothpick inserted into center comes out clean. Cool completely.

In medium bowl, mix frosting and peanut butter until smooth. Spread evenly over cake. Sprinkle with peanuts and candy bar. Arrange candy pumpkins on cake.

HALLOWEEN SPIDER CAKE

Cake:

> 1 **white cake mix**
> 1 small box **lime gelatin**

Frosting:

> **blue food coloring**
> **chocolate frosting**

Decorations:

> 4 pieces **black licorice**
> 2 **large green gumballs**

Prepare lime gelatin as directed on the box; refrigerate.

Prepare cake batter according to package directions. Bake in two 9-inch round cake pans.

Cut a smaller circle out of the center of one cake. Set it aside for the head. Fill the hole with prepared gelatin that has been chopped up into small pieces. Lay the other cake on top. Place the small circle at head of big circle. Add blue food coloring to chocolate frosting until black in color; cover cake with frosting. Use black licorice as legs and gumballs as eyes.

PUMPKIN DELIGHT

Crust:

1 **yellow cake mix** (reserve one cup for topping)
1 stick **margarine**, melted
1 **egg**

Filling:

1 can (29 ounces) **pumpkin**
2 **eggs**
$^2/_3$ cup **milk**
1 cup **sugar**
1 teaspoon **cinnamon**
$^1/_2$ teaspoon **nutmeg**
$^1/_2$ teaspoon **ginger**
$^1/_2$ teaspoon **salt**

Topping:

1 cup **reserved cake mix**
2 tablespoons **sugar**
$^1/_2$ stick **margarine**

Preheat oven to 350 degrees.

To make crust, combine cake mix (minus 1 cup), melted margarine, and egg. Press into a greased 9 x 13-inch pan.

Combine all filling ingredients and mix until smooth. Pour over crust.

For topping, mix reserved cake mix, cinnamon, and sugar; cut in margarine until crumbly. Sprinkle over filling.

Bake 50 minutes, or until a knife inserted into center comes out clean.

PEPPERMINT CAKE

Cake:

> 1 **white cake mix**
> ³/₄ cup **water**
> 2 **egg whites**
> ¹/₃ cup **vegetable oil**
> ¹/₂ cup **crushed peppermint candy**

Topping:

> 1 can (16 ounces) **vanilla frosting**
> 2 ¹/₂ tablespoons **crushed peppermint candy**

Preheat oven to 350 degrees.

In a large bowl, combine cake mix, water, egg whites, and oil until smooth. Stir in ¹/₂ cup crushed candy. Pour batter into a greased 9 x 13-inch pan.

Bake 25 to 35 minutes, or until golden brown. Cool completely.

Spread frosting over cooked cake; sprinkle with crushed candy.

CHRISTMAS-RAINBOW POKE CAKE

1 **white cake mix**
1 small box **strawberry gelatin**
1 small box **lime gelatin**
2 cups **boiling water**, divided
$1/2$ cup **cold water**, divided
12 ounces **whipped topping**, thawed

Prepare cake mix as directed on package. Pour batter into two 8- or 9-inch round pans, and bake as directed; cool 10 minutes. Remove from pans; cool completely.

Place cake layers, top sides up, back in the two clean pans. With a fork, poke holes at 1-inch intervals through both cakes.

Dissolve strawberry gelatin into 1 cup boiling water. Mix $1/4$-cup cold water into gelatin. Spoon over one layer. Repeat with lime gelatin. Refrigerate 3–4 hours or overnight.

Dip one pan into warm water 10 seconds; invert on serving plate. Cover the layer with part of the whipped topping. Invert second layer onto first layer. Frost with remaining topping. Refrigerate.

ABOUT THE AUTHOR

Stephanie Dircks Ashcraft was raised near Kirklin, Indiana. She received a bachelor's degree in family science and a teaching certificate from Brigham Young University. She teaches a monthly cooking class entitled "101 Things to Do with a Cake Mix" for Macey's Little Cooking Theater in Provo and Orem, Utah. She and her husband, Ivan Ashcraft, are the parents of two young children, Devan and Elizabeth. Being a mom is her full-time job.